I0605207

BELLWETHER MEDIA • MINNEAPOLIS, MN

Blastoff! Readers are carefully developed by literacy experts to build reading stamina and move students toward fluency by combining standards-based content with developmentally appropriate text.

Level 1 provides the most support through repetition of high-frequency words, light text, predictable sentence patterns, and strong visual support.

Level 2 offers early readers a bit more challenge through varied sentences, increased text load, and text-supportive special features.

Level 3 advances early-fluent readers toward fluency through increased text load, less reliance on photos, advancing concepts, longer sentences, and more complex special features.

★ **Blastoff! Universe**

Reading Level

Grade K

Grades 1–3

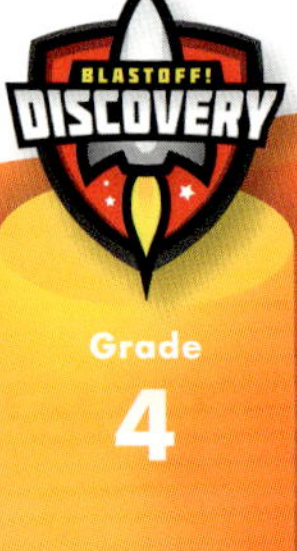

Grade 4

This edition first published in 2025 by Bellwether Media, Inc.

Library of Congress Cataloging-in-Publication Data

LC record for Snowy Owls available at: https://lccn.loc.gov/2024000762

Editor: Christina Leaf   Series Designer: Brittany McIntosh   Book Designer: Veah Demmin

Printed in the United States of America, North Mankato, MN.

Table of Contents

At Home in the Snow

Snowy owls live mostly in the **Arctic**. They blend in with their frozen home.

These owls have many feathers. They keep their bodies warm.

Snowy owls are large. They can be over 2 feet (0.6 meters) tall.

Their **wingspan** can reach nearly 5 feet (1.5 meters) wide!

0 1 foot 2 feet 3 feet 4 feet 5 feet

nearly 5 feet (1.5 meters) wide

Snowy owls have round heads. Their black beaks are sharp.

Their white faces have
bright yellow eyes.

Dark spots dot the owls' white bodies. Females have many dark spots. Males grow whiter with age.

White feathers cover their legs and even their feet!

Daytime Hunters

Snowy owls live in open areas of snow and ice. They hunt during the day.

They often fly low to the ground.

Snowy owls usually eat small **mammals**. They catch **prey** with their sharp **talons**.

They have excellent hearing. They can find prey hidden underneath snow!

Snowy owls **protect** their homes. They puff out their feathers and flap their wings. Other owls stay away!

Snowy owls dive to attack **predators**.

Growing Up!

Many snowy owls **migrate** south for the winter. Pairs **mate** in late spring.

Females make nests on the ground. They lay bigger **clutches** when there is plenty to eat.

Owlets come out of their eggs in 32 days. They are fluffy.

Soon owlets grow adult feathers. They become **fledglings**. They learn to fly!

fledgling

Growing Up

owlets

Glossary

Arctic—the cold, frozen land and seas around the North Pole

clutches—groups of eggs that are laid together

fledglings—young owls that have feathers for flight

mammals—warm-blooded animals that have backbones and feed their young milk

mate—to join together to make young

migrate—to travel from one place to another, often with the seasons

owlets—baby owls

predators—animals that hunt other animals for food

prey—animals that are hunted by other animals for food

protect—to keep safe

talons—the strong, sharp claws of owls and other raptors

wingspan—the distance from the tip of one wing to the tip of the other wing

To Learn More

AT THE LIBRARY

Grack, Rachel. *Snowy Owls.* Minneapolis, Minn.: Bellwether Media, 2024.

Porter, Jane. *So You Want to Be an Owl.* Somerville, Mass.: Candlewick Press, 2021.

Rustad, Martha E.H. *Animals of the Arctic Tundra.* North Mankato, Minn.: Pebble, 2022.

ON THE WEB

FACTSURFER

Factsurfer.com gives you a safe, fun way to find more information.

1. Go to www.factsurfer.com.
2. Enter "snowy owls" into the search box and click 🔍.
3. Select your book cover to see a list of related content.

Index

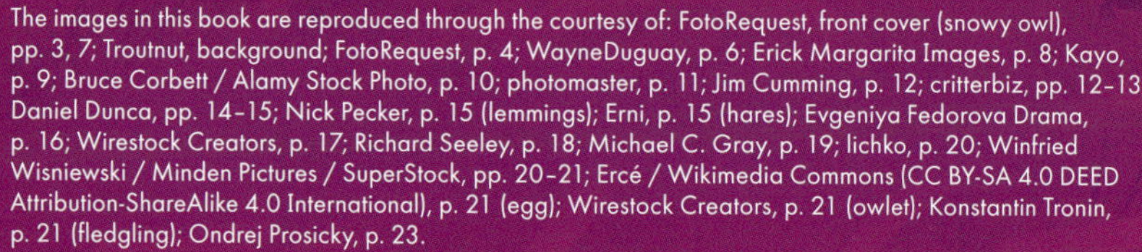

The images in this book are reproduced through the courtesy of: FotoRequest, front cover (snowy owl), pp. 3, 7; Troutnut, background; FotoRequest, p. 4; WayneDuguay, p. 6; Erick Margarita Images, p. 8; Kayo, p. 9; Bruce Corbett / Alamy Stock Photo, p. 10; photomaster, p. 11; Jim Cumming, p. 12; critterbiz, pp. 12–13; Daniel Dunca, pp. 14–15; Nick Pecker, p. 15 (lemmings); Erni, p. 15 (hares); Evgeniya Fedorova Drama, p. 16; Wirestock Creators, p. 17; Richard Seeley, p. 18; Michael C. Gray, p. 19; lichko, p. 20; Winfried Wisniewski / Minden Pictures / SuperStock, pp. 20–21; Ercé / Wikimedia Commons (CC BY-SA 4.0 DEED Attribution-ShareAlike 4.0 International), p. 21 (egg); Wirestock Creators, p. 21 (owlet); Konstantin Tronin, p. 21 (fledgling); Ondrej Prosicky, p. 23.